Contents:

For my father
who spent a lifetime with Luther

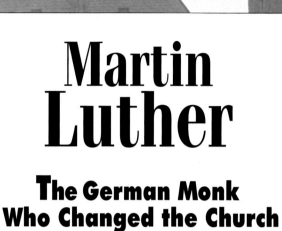

Martin Luther

The German Monk
Who Changed the Church

1483 — 1546

Great men and women are not in need of our praise.
We are the ones in need of getting to know them.

By Ben Alex

Illustrations by Giuseppe Rava

VICTOR BOOKS

A DIVISION OF SCRIPTURE PRESS PUBLICATIONS INC.
USA CANADA ENGLAND

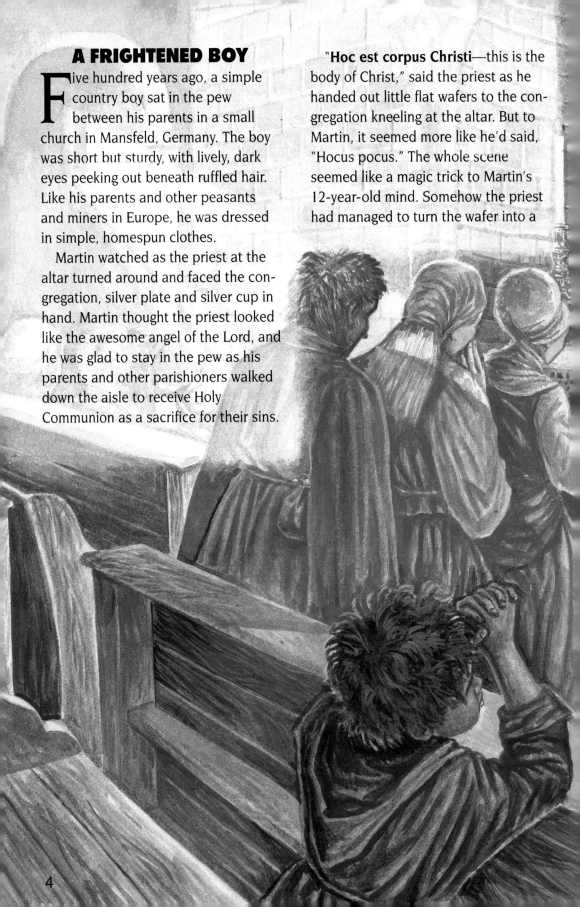

A FRIGHTENED BOY

Five hundred years ago, a simple country boy sat in the pew between his parents in a small church in Mansfeld, Germany. The boy was short but sturdy, with lively, dark eyes peeking out beneath ruffled hair. Like his parents and other peasants and miners in Europe, he was dressed in simple, homespun clothes.

Martin watched as the priest at the altar turned around and faced the congregation, silver plate and silver cup in hand. Martin thought the priest looked like the awesome angel of the Lord, and he was glad to stay in the pew as his parents and other parishioners walked down the aisle to receive Holy Communion as a sacrifice for their sins.

"**Hoc est corpus Christi**—this is the body of Christ," said the priest as he handed out little flat wafers to the congregation kneeling at the altar. But to Martin, it seemed more like he'd said, "Hocus pocus." The whole scene seemed like a magic trick to Martin's 12-year-old mind. Somehow the priest had managed to turn the wafer into a

piece of Christ's body! Martin wondered what it would look like and taste like as the priest put the bread into his mother's mouth. What did it do to her when she swallowed it?

Martin looked up at the high altar and shuddered. Above it he could see the triangle with the eye of God in the middle—the disapproving eye he could never escape. What kind of God was this? Why had He sacrificed His own Son Jesus and sent pieces of His Body around the world so people could swallow them Sunday after Sunday at Mass? If God had treated His own beloved Son in this horrible way, how would He treat someone like Martin, who had done so many bad things that his parents and teachers had to cane him several times a week?

Martin thought he hated God. He was afraid of Him, too. Martin was confused. He didn't know what to think. The only thing he knew for sure was that he was a wicked person who needed someone to help him escape hell and reach heaven. God was stern and remote—at least that's what he imagined. Jesus, God's Son, was the righteous Judge of all people; Martin didn't think he could count on mercy from Him either. Then there was Mary, Jesus' mother. She seemed too pious and holy for Martin. His only hope seemed to be the saints—especially St. Anne, the mother of Mary. She was the patroness of miners, and Martin's father was a miner. Maybe St. Anne would put in a good word for him at the judgment throne of God.

Martin looked up at the paintings on the church wall and shrugged again. There were monks—bishops even—being tortured by monsters and vampires in purgatory. There were people being dragged off to hell by devils with claws and pitchforks. There were saints being beheaded with the sword for their firm faith in God. On the ceiling was painted a picture of Christ on a rainbow, surrounded by angels with trumpets. From Christ's right ear grew a lily, from his left ear a sword. Martin knew that the lily meant grace and forgiveness; the sword, judgment and damnation. How could Martin earn the lily and avoid the sword? He thought about it all during the Church service.

The late Middle Ages was a time of discovery and adventure, but people's minds were controlled by superstition and fear of evil.

Europe Changes

Martin Luther grew up in the period of great change between the Middle Ages and what we now call the Renaissance. For over a thousand years Europe had been dominated by what had been a wealthy Catholic Church. Anyone who spoke against the teaching and policies of the Church risked being burned at the stake. Among peasants of that time, the only hope for a reasonably good life was to obey what Church leaders said and patiently wait for heaven.

But at the time of Luther's birth in 1483, the Church had serious problems. It was nearly bankrupt. Its power was crumbling. Emperors, princes and nobles were securing the land and influence which had once belonged to the

Church. Universities sprang up, breaking the Church's monopoly on education. New ideas about life began to take shape as artists like Leonardo da Vinci and Michelangelo, and scholars and scientists like Erasmus of Rotterdam and Copernicus showed there were other ways of thinking.

Adventurers explored the earth beyond the boundaries set by the Church centuries before. When Luther was five years old, the Portuguese rounded the southern tip of Africa for the first time (1488) and opened up the sea clear to the Orient. When Luther was nine, Christopher Columbus crossed the Atlantic Ocean and discovered the continent known as North America. These discoveries and others made it plain that the Church had been wrong about many scientific questions. The earth was not flat, after all. Neither was it the center of the universe, as the Church had taught people to believe.

New knowledge about the world spread quickly due to the first mass media invention in history: Gutenberg's printing press (around 1450).

But young Luther was not impressed by the newest artistic or scientific ideas or the latest inventions. He had grown up among simple folk, fighting poverty and sickness just like them. He had a quick mind and curious nature, and he believed firmly in the traditional authority of the Church. Gradually, his personal study of God's Word changed the way he thought about the Church. His beliefs and opinions were published widely via the printing press and began to influence the culture of the day. Without knowing it, Martin Luther changed the history of the Church and its impact throughout the world.

PRINCE, EMPEROR AND POPE

Once outside, after Mass, Martin felt better. The green hills of Thuringia were blooming with flowers. He could smell the moist earth and feel the sun on his back. A lark fluttered above, singing a song for spring. Swallows flew north from far-away Africa to the blue skies of Scandinavia. A fawn watched him curiously from a distance.

"Sir, look!" cried Martin to his father as he pointed to the castle outside Mansfeld. At that moment the heavy iron gate was opening and out rode a knight dressed in a velvet jacket and plumed hat, riding a black horse. Three servants followed. They wore crimson-colored vests with purple trim and yellow-striped hose. The horses' silver trappings jingled.

"Take off your hat, Martin!" warned his father. "It's the Count of Mansfeld."

The count and his men galloped by, startling a nearby rabbit. Then they disappeared over a hill. In passing, the count shouted, "Guten Tag, Hans Luder!" Martin's father felt proud and waved. Martin felt proud too.

"You know the count, sir?" he asked admiringly.

"Yes," smiled his father. Then he added, "And you'll know him too, if you follow in my footsteps. You may even become an overseer of the count's copper mines!"

"Sir, who is more important than the count?" wondered Martin. "The emperor?"

"No," answered his father, "the count is under the authority of Prince Frederick, Elector of Saxony, and the prince is under Emperor Maximilian, lord of the Holy Roman Empire. The country of Germany is part of that empire."

"Is the pope over the emperor then?"

"No. The pope is the great lord of the Church. The emperor is lord of the world."

"We must obey both the emperor and the pope, is that right?" questioned Martin.

"Yes," nodded Hans. "Any disobedience to the pope means excommunication from the Church and eternity in hell. Disobedience to the emperor means punishment and sometimes death. Just look over there!" Hans pointed.

Martin shuddered at the sight of the gallows. In one of them still hung the lifeless body of a peasant. Martin remembered the stocks in the marketplace, where he'd often seen people being held for days.

"That's why a child must learn to obey his parents," said Martin's mother. "If not, the count may come and take you to the dungeons."

A STRANGE BEGGAR

Martin was almost 14 when his father came home one day from the smelting furnace in the mines and said, "Son, you're a smart lad. I've been thinking you ought to have a good education and become a learned man instead of a miner. I want you to become a lawyer so you can support your mother and me in our old age."

Martin beamed as his father added, "It's time we sent you to a better school. I've arranged for you to spend the next term at the Franciscan school in Magdeburg."

A week later Martin waved goodbye to his parents and his younger brothers and sisters and set out for Magdeburg, forty miles north of Mansfeld. With him was his friend Johann.

Martin loved his new school. The teachers were not as harsh as his teachers in Mansfeld, and he soon advanced in his studies. His teachers noticed his thirst for learning.

One day after school, when Martin and Johann went door to door to beg for food—as was customary at the Latin school in Magdeburg—they noticed a lonely beggar staggering down the street. The beggar carried a bag of food on his back. He looked like moving bones—a bent skeleton in a monk's robe.

Martin stopped. "Who's that?" he exclaimed.

Luther's Early Life

Luther's birthplace in Eisleben

I'm the son of a peasant," Luther liked to say. Luther's great-grandfather, grandfather and father, Hans Luder, were all farmers. Hans did not inherit his family's farm, however, because custom dictated the youngest son should have it. So Hans went to the city to seek his fortune in the copper mines. He became a hard-working miner, prospered and bought two mines of his own. He was a well-to-do middle-class citizen by the time his son Martin became a monk.

Hans and Margaretha, Luther's mother, had at least five children (Martin was the oldest). The couple disciplined their children for the smallest offences. Once, Martin's mother caned him "until the blood came" for taking a nut without asking. Another time his father beat him so he ran away and "felt ugly toward him." "Although they meant well,"

"Aye, that's William of Anhalt," said a passerby. "William was once a wealthy prince, but he gave everything up to seek God and become a monk. He's a very saintly man. He fasts and prays whenever he's not begging food for his fellow monks."

Martin stared after the monk as he turned down another street. Then he said to Johann, "I wish I were holy. Maybe God would love me if I were as holy as Prince William."

Luther said later, "it was discipline like this that finally drove me to the monastery." There, he found the balance between strictness and grace he was seeking.

Some biographers suggest Luther's arguments against the Catholic Church may have been linked to the harsh punishment he received from his stern parents. However, there is every reason to believe Martin also received from Hans and Margaretha the love necessary to foster self-esteem, which enabled him to break with the authority of the Church.

Luther's parents, Hans and Margaretha Luder. Painted by Luther's friend, Lucas Granach.

HAPPY DAYS IN EISENACH

A year went by. Martin's father sent him to a better school further from home. At first Martin was sad to leave his friends at Magdeburg. But in Eisenach he found new friends and didn't have to beg for his supper. His father could now afford to pay tuition as well as a small allowance, and he had arranged for relatives to look after his son occasionally.

The Latin school at St. George's Church in Eisenach was no ordinary school. The students learned, not out of fear of punishment as in the other schools, but for love of knowledge. The school principal, Master Trebonius, would remove his scholar's cap in the classroom and address the students as "sirs." And he required his teachers to do the same.

"The students on these benches," he would say, "are the future mayors, chancellors, doctors and rulers of Germany."

Martin blossomed in this new environment. By now he had mastered the difficult Latin language, while also mak-

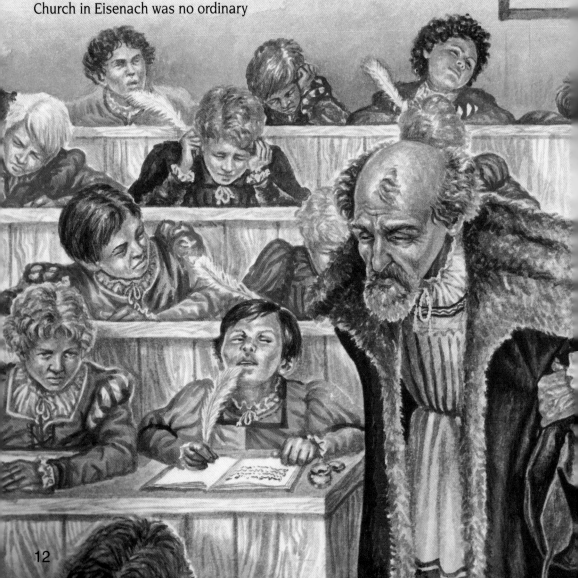

ing exceptional progress in other languages and literature. At a party in honor of a visiting professor, Master Trebonius chose Martin to make the official welcome speech—in Latin.

"Keep an eye on this lad," whispered the professor to Trebonius during the speech. "Prepare him well for the university. He will go far in life."

Frau Cotta, a merry, wealthy woman, had given Martin free room and board in return for helping her little son with his homework. Musicians, artists and pious priests were regular visitors at the Cotta house, and Martin basked in their conversations. He learned to play the lute and studied various musical disciplines.

After three years in Eisenach, Martin walked north to visit his parents in Mansfeld. Once outside Eisenach, he turned and took one last look at its beauty along the Elbe river, with the castle of Wartburg towering above it.

"This is my favorite place," he thought, "and always will be, even if I should live a hundred years!"

HIGH GOALS FOR MARTIN

Hans and Margaretha Luder were thrilled to see their oldest son again. How tall he'd grown! How deep his voice had become! How smart he seemed! Hans couldn't help returning the respect he'd always demanded from Martin.

"Sir," Hans said with pride in his voice, "you certainly look like a real scholar!" Then he handed Martin a present he had long wanted to give him: a complete set of law books called **Corpus Juris Civilis**. As he watched the look of surprise on his son's face, he added, "You'll need them. Martin, I want you to go to the university at Erfurt!"

"And another thing," said his moth- er from behind, "you'll need a good and able wife. We've already been talking to a wealthy family . . . ."

THE CROWN OF LEARNING

Erfurt was a beautiful and prosper- ous city fifty miles south of Mansfeld. The forest sloped down into gentle hills covered with orchards and vineyards, while green-blue-yellow fields of indigo, flax and saffronon grew on the other side of the city. In the midst of this beautiful German land- scape rose the walls and steeples of the many-spired city.

To walk through the city gate was to enter the promised land of the highest education on offer at that time. The university at Erfurt made other universi-

ties in Germany seem like elementary schools. After four years of further study, Martin, nicknamed "The Philosopher" by his many friends, had received a Master of Arts degree, ranking second out of a class of seventeen.

"A few more years of hard study," he thought as he and the other graduates rode through the crowds of cheering citizens, "and I'll be a prominent lawyer with the whole world at my feet! Mother and Father will be so proud of me!"

But then something happened which would alter Martin's promising career forever, and bring to ruin the high hopes of his parents.

A TERRIBLE THUNDERSTORM

One sultry July afternoon in 1505, as 21-year-old Martin was walking back to Erfurt after a ten-day visit with his parents, he was overwhelmed by childhood fears of God and death. There had been a series of dark events in his life. The Black Plague had struck Erfurt. Shortly before, a close friend had died from typhoid fever along with many other people, all behind doors painted with black crosses. Martin himself had nearly died following an accident with his sword. Now, on his way back to his law studies, he felt terrified as thoughts of God's anger and punishment coarsed through his mind.

Such fears were common to people in the Middle Ages, provoked partly by the Roman Catholic Church, where Martin had received his religious training. In order to control the lay people, the clergy stirred the fear of hell in them as a way of driving them to the sacraments of the Church. The sacraments and confession raised hope for God's forgiveness through penance. The Church's teaching on purgatory as a place between heaven and hell with

15

temporary torment for those not bad enough for hell, nor good enough for heaven, nurtured new fear of death. The Church helped overcome this fear by promising to reduce time in purgatory if people gave money to the Church and prayed to the saints.

The picture of the beggar prince from his Magdeburg days flashed through Martin's mind. How could he become holy and earn the mercy of God? How could he be rid of his sin and sure of going to heaven—not purgatory, when he died?

Suddenly Martin was interrupted in his thoughts. The blue sky had turned

black with clouds. Torrents of rain began pouring down. A lightning bolt hit a nearby tree and split it in half. Terror filled Martin's eyes as he sought shelter from the thunderstorm. Another bolt knocked him to the ground. He thought it must be the bolt of wrath from an angry God! Martin raised his head from the mud and cried out, "Saint Anne! Help me! If you spare me, I promise I shall become a godly monk!"

MARTIN BECOMES A MONK

Martin did survive that storm. Back in Erfurt, he kept his vow. Two weeks after the thunderstorm he left the university for the monastery. His friends all tried to talk him out of the plan, but in vain. Martin had already given away his Corpus Juris books and written a letter to his father, explaining his decision to give up a worldly career. Martin's mind was set. He would become a monk by making the threefold vow of poverty, chastity and obedience to God and the Catholic Church!

On the morning of July 17th, 1505, the gates of the Augustinian monastery in Erfurt closed behind him. That same day he was received as a novice into the order, at a ceremony in the chapel.

"Do you know what your decision means?" asked the prior from the altar. Then he quickly added, "This means poverty, rough clothing, a scant diet and the shame of begging! It means dying to yourself, abstinence from worldly desires, vigils by night and labors by day, daily confessions, constant prayer, and the loneliness of monastery life! Are you willing to take such burdens upon yourself?"

"Yes, with God's help," answered Martin, "as He gives me strength."

Then the crown of Martin's head was shaved into the tonsure of a holy man. He was stripped of his fine student's clothing in front of the friars and given the hair shirt and simple robe of a monk.

19

SEEKING GOD IN A MONK'S CELL

Life in the monastery was more difficult than Martin had expected. Not only was he given the hardest labor to perform, he also had to deal with the suspicion and jealousy of friars less educated and less zealous than himself. But Brother Martin threw himself wholeheartedly into the pious lifestyle of the strict monastery. He starved himself and spent hours lying on the floor in his cell, arms stretched out in the shape of a cross. By night he threw off his allotted blankets and froze himself to sleep. Every morning at 2 a.m. he got up to say his first prayers. Day and night he brooded over past sins and spent hours confessing them to the prior. But in spite of his determination to please God, the self-tormenting monk did not gain

"I was a good monk, and I kept the rule of my order so strictly that I may say that if ever a monk got to heaven by his monkery it was I."—Luther

20

peace in his heart.

One day, when the rector of the Augustinian order, Dr. Staupitz, was visiting the monastery, he took the zealous friar for a walk in the garden.

"Brother Martin," began Staupitz, "you're making religion too difficult. You can't impress God by trying to become perfect. All you must do is love Him."

"Love Him?" exclaimed Martin. "Father, how can I love a God who's angry with me?"

The old rector stopped and put a hand on Martin's shoulder. "God is not angry with you," he gently said, "it's you who are angry with God! You're trying to find sins in yourself instead of trusting that God loved you first. He proved it by sending Jesus to die for your sins!" Then he added, "Brother Martin, I have a new task for you. Instead of tormenting yourself with the confession of your sins, I want you to teach at the university in Erfurt . . . and I want you to become a priest!"

"A priest?" gasped Martin.

"Yes," repeated Staupitz, "a priest who will preach for others and administer the sacraments of the Church."

"No!" protested Martin. "I am too sinful. I could never do that! I think I should die!"

"Well," replied the old man with a twinkle in his eye, "do you suppose God will wait until heaven to make use of clever men like you?"

MARTIN
BECOMES A PRIEST

Martin studied harder than ever to prepare for the priesthood. He learned the liturgy of the Church by heart. He spent many hours reading the large Bible on the stand in the dining hall until he was finally given a red leather Bible of his own. This gift meant a hundred times more to him than the law books he had received from his father.

On April 3rd, 1507, Martin was ordained as a priest. A month later he was to say his first Mass. Yet, he still remained as unsure of his heavenly Father's acceptance as he was of his earthly father's.

For Hans Luder had not seen his son since he had become a monk almost two years earlier. Now old Hans was sitting in the monastery chapel watching the ceremony.

Martin performed his duties at the altar and faced the congregation of honored guests and distinguished scholars, cup and plate in hand. He seemed calm. But no one could know that in his head a tiny voice whispered, "Martin, you'll never make it! You're not worthy to be a priest. This is blasphemy! How are you going to transform the bread and wine into the Body of Christ? Instead you'll drop it on the floor! You'll desecrate God's Gift with obscene words! Look, your father is watching you. He'll never accept you!"

Martin raised his head and brushed the voice of doubt aside. He noticed a gentle smile on Dr. Staupitz' face. Then he distributed the bread to the altar guests. As his father opened his mouth to receive the Body of Christ, Martin looked him in the eye and smiled. He knew he was doing something important beyond his father's opinion of him.

"**Hoc est corpus Christi**," he said and placed the bread on the tip of Hans Luder's tongue.

Later, at the celebration in the dining hall, Martin greeted his father, hoping for a word of encouragement. But old Hans was grave and quiet.

"Father," said Martin, "today I'm a priest! Why didn't you want this? Life here is so quiet and godly!"

Hans Luder had long tried to suppress his disappointment in his son's decision. Martin's innocent question was too much, though, and old anger welled up inside him. In front of all those monks and educated guests Hans burst out, "You learned scholar, haven't you read the Bible enough to know you are to honor your father and mother? See what you've done! You've left your parents to look after themselves in their old age!"

"But father," replied Martin with a confidence that surprised even him, "the Bible also tells us to forsake our father and mother and follow Christ. You know He called me through a thunderstorm to become a monk!"

"God grant it wasn't the devil!" snarled Hans Luder.

Luther's First Doubts

While Martin Luther was a priest in Erfurt, Germany, his supervisor sent him on a business trip to Rome. Luther was excited to be chosen for the trip. He could hardly wait to see the places held sacred by the Church, especially the new St. Peter's basilica and the Scala Santa stairs, believed to be the stairs Jesus climbed on His way to crucifixion.

Outside the city, Luther fell on his knees and exclaimed, "Hail, Holy Rome, you glorious city where the blood of the martyrs was spilled!"

But Rome was not as holy as Luther had expected. During his four-week stay he was shocked by the poor morals, language and behavior of Church officials. He heard stories about the rich luxury in the pope's court, all paid for with money taken from poor farmers. He heard jokes making fun of the sacraments, told by priests who were supposed to love and honor God. Even the monks openly ridiculed the saints respected by Luther.

But even in Rome, Martin Luther did not lose his faith in the Church. He prayed in Roman chapels where relics of the martyrs and saints were displayed. He climbed the stairs of Scala Santa on his knees, saying the Lord's Prayer on every step and believing, as he'd been taught, that a soul would be released from purgatory when he was done. But when Luther arrived at the top step, he was suddenly overcome by doubt. He turned to a friend and said, "Who knows if this is really true?"

This flash of doubt in Church authority stayed with Luther all the way home to Erfurt. He began to study God's

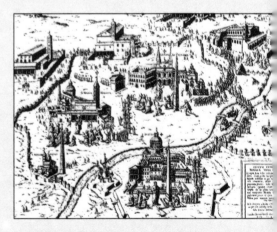

Word more eagerly than ever and eventually came to realize no one is able to receive eternal life for himself—or for anybody else—by doing good works.

LUTHER THE LEADER

Time proved old Hans wrong. Six years after Martin had said his first Mass, he became Dr. Martinus Lutherus, a respected Doctor of Theology, subprior in the monastery, district-vicar of the order, after Dr. Staupitz, and a popular professor at the new university in Wittenberg.

Compared with beautiful Erfurt, Wittenberg was an insignificant village of 2,000 people. Situated on a barren sand dune along the Elbe river, it seemed on the edge of civilization. But the elector of Saxony, Prince Frederick the Wise, had his residence here—and Frederick had big plans for his hometown.

First, Frederick wanted to make Wittenberg the most prestigious center of learning and education in Germany. For this purpose he needed a modern university with brilliant professors. Second, he wanted to turn Wittenberg into a famous place of worship for pilgrims. His remarkable collection of relics, or sacred objects, was exhibited at the castle church and drew pilgrims from all over; more than 5,000 relics, including a twig from Moses' burning bush, a thorn from the crown of Christ and a tooth from the holy church father, St. Jerome. Pilgrims who saw the relics and paid a coin to the Church were given an indulgence —a piece of paper signed by the pope guaranteeing forgiveness of sins and reduction of time for loved ones in purgatory. A successful pilgrimage to Wittenberg could reduce purgatory time by 1,443 years.

Martin Luther was a frequent preacher in the castle church. But he didn't like the way people worshiped the relics and saints in order to gain forgiveness of their sins. He wished they could worship God and repent of their sins, rather than looking to pay their way out of it!

The people of Wittenberg liked Luther. Here was an honest man, they felt, who went right to the heart of

things—practical, not theoretical like most other preachers. He didn't try to impress the educated. He cared for the common man, and bravely spoke out against Church abuse of people's sincere devotion and religious fears.

As a university professor, Luther was admired for his straightforward teaching methods. Though Latin was the required classroom language, Luther often used common German phrases—just as we use slang today—in order to bring the Bible to life in the hearts of his students. Once, a colleague exclaimed, "This man will completely revolutionize the teaching of theology!"

THE DARK
NIGHT OF THE SOUL

Even as a university professor, however, Luther still struggled with the fearsome God of his childhood. Night after night, as Wittenberg slept, he continued to sit at the heavy wooden table in the tower of the Black Cloister, the monastery where he lived. In front of him the light of a candle flickered across the pages of a worn Bible.

"God, how can I know You?" he whispered into the darkness. "How can I love You?"

"Ha," he seemed to hear a voice mocking him, "what are you praying for? Just see how quiet it is around you. Do you think God hears your prayers and would pay attention to a sinner like you?"

Luther's eyes sought the candle, then fell on the section in the Book of Psalms he was preparing for the next morning's lecture. Suddenly a sentence jumped out at him, "My God, my God, why hast thou forsaken me?"

Wasn't this the cry of Christ on the cross? What could this mean? Could it mean that Jesus, the Son of God, had once felt abandoned and forsaken by God, also? Had Jesus suffered torment

"I felt myself
to be reborn and
to have gone
through open doors
into paradise."
—Luther

and abandonment? Was it because of sin? No. Jesus was without sin. Why then? Luther wondered.

The answer came like a flash of light into Luther's dark soul: Jesus had taken upon Himself the sufferings of sinners! On the cross He had carried the sins of the world!

A heavy load fell from Luther's mind. In an instant the burden of sin and condemnation lifted. A smile crept over the shadows of his face as he turned to the words from St. Paul's letter to the Romans that had puzzled him for so long, "The righteous shall live by faith."

Those words had made him tremble with fear in the past, for he was far from righteous. Now, in the light of the cross, Luther realized Jesus had suffered the punishment for his sin so that he could receive the righteousness of Jesus as a free gift. God had declared him righteous and without sin in Jesus. To trust God for this was to live by faith!

That night, in the cloister tower in Wittenberg, Luther felt at peace because he knew that a God who gives His own Son as a sacrifice for sin is not an angry, but a loving God.

Luther had found the lily of grace.

TETZEL'S TRUNK

There were rumors in town. Pope Leo X, the head of the Catholic Church, had pronounced a special jubilee year. By offering a generous contribution to the Church during this year of jubilee, people could purchase an indulgence, or letter of credit, signed by the pope himself. An indulgence letter promised immediate forgiveness of past sins and reduction of time for loved ones in purgatory.

Ordinarily people would have been excited because this meant they could secure the afterlife for themselves and their families. But people were becoming increasingly angry. They thought the pope and the German archbishop had invented the idea in order to raise money to pay off their debts and finish the new St. Peter's Cathedral in Rome. Yet no one dared speak out against them.

The pope's messengers traveled throughout Europe, carrying letters of indulgence. The most well-known messenger, the monk Johann Tetzel, approached a town not far from Wittenberg. He entered the town in a spectacular religious parade, preceded by the cross with the pope's coat of arms, and the bull of indulgence on a gold-embroidered velvet cushion.

The cross was planted in the marketplace. Tetzel preached a masterful sermon that played on the fears of the common people:

"Now, listen to the voices of your

> "Christ did not command the preaching of indulgences but of the gospel."
>
> —Luther

dear dead relatives and friends! They are begging you, 'Pity us! Pity us! We're in terrible torment! Only you can save us. All it takes is your small contribution!' Why don't you help them? Open your ears! Hear parents cry to their children, 'We gave birth to you, we nourished you and raised you! We left you our inheritance! Why are you so cruel that you won't save us now? Will you leave us here in flames forever? Will you really delay our entry to heaven?'"

After the sermon Tetzel opened his money trunk with a little chant:

"Once the coin into the coffer clings,
The soul from purgatory heavenward springs!"

People flocked around Tetzel's trunk. Some of Luther's parishioners were among those who threw in coins to receive the pope's official letters of indulgence.

LUTHER GOES PUBLIC

When one of these letters was shown to Luther, he thundered, "This peddler thinks he can bargain with God's forgiveness!" Luther stamped on the letter. "This indulgence thing has gone too far. It has to be stopped!" Then he turned and disappeared into his study.

On the Eve of All Saints, October 31st, 1517, Luther marched out of the Black Cloister gate towards the castle church. In his hands he held a poster, a hammer and some nails. He was spotted by a couple of university students who then followed him. The professor stopped in front of the heavy church door, the town's official bulletin board. Then he nailed the poster to the door and marched back towards the Augustinian monastery.

"Look," said the one student as he glanced at the poster, "Dr. Luther is protesting against indulgences!"

"Goodness," answered the other, "he has written 95 arguments in Latin!"

"Prince Frederick won't like this!" continued the first. "All Saints' Day is the only day of the year the prince has permission to sell indulgences in Wittenberg. Now Luther is protesting against this business."

"And the prince needs money to run the university. Luther is in trouble!"

"But he's right, isn't he? Isn't it scandalous that people are taught they can be saved by paying money to the prince and the pope?"

"You can say that again! Dr. Luther says it's an abuse of God's grace."

The Poster on the Church Door

The 95 theses were Luther's reasons for questioning the Church's trafficking in indulgences. The poster was printed by a local man who kept a copy for himself. Within two weeks the theses were reprinted and distributed throughout Germany, without Luther's permission. Within another two weeks they had been translated and were being read all over Europe.

Six months later, Luther wrote to Pope Leo X, "It is a mystery to me how my theses were spread to so many places. They were meant only for local academic debate."

Little did Luther know they would eventually become the declaration of independence for the reformation movement that broke with the Catholic Church.

The following are some of Luther's theses:

- When our Lord and Master, Jesus Christ, says "Repent," He means the entire life of the faithful should be a repentance.

- They preach human folly who pretend that as soon as a coin in the coffer clings, the soul from purgatory heavenward springs.

- Those who suppose that on account of their letters of indulgence they are sure of salvation will be eternally damned along with their teachers.

- Christians should be taught that whoever sees a person in need and, instead of helping him, uses his money for an indulgence, obtains not an indulgence of the pope but the displeasure of God.

- Christians should be taught that the pope ought and would give his own goods to the poor . . . even if he had to sell St. Peter's Cathedral to do it.

- Let them set their trust on entering heaven through many tribulations rather than some false security and peace.

The Wittenberg Castle Church

ORDERED TO ROME

Pope Leo put the books back on his secretary's desk and said, "These writings by Martinus Luther sound like the words of a drunk German monk!".

Pope Leo did not like what he had read. He did not like Church authority to be questioned, because that was to question his own authority as head of it.

Emperor Maximilian, head of the Holy Roman Empire which covered most of Europe, did not like Luther's writings either. He felt Luther might incite a revolution against the government. Besides, Maximilian needed the Church's moral support. "We must stop this monk immediately," he wrote Pope Leo, "before the German people and princes follow him."

Pope Leo had an official document drafted, making it a law that people show absolute loyalty to the teachings of the Church. This made Luther's writings a criminal offense. It stated, "Anyone who questions the teaching of the Church and the pope in all matters of faith is a heretic."

When Luther learned about Leo's document, he became furious. He realized Church authorities were only interested in protecting themselves, not in seeking the truth or looking to God for help. Luther had hoped for a worthy debate that would stop the indul-

> "I have great hope, that as Christ was rejected by the Jews and received by the Gentiles, so this true theology, rejected by opinionated old men, will pass over to the younger generation."
>
> —Luther

gence trade. Instead, he had become trapped in a political power game and been declared a heretic.

A letter with the pope's seal arrived at Luther's door. Luther was ordered to appear before a court in Rome within sixty days. He was being charged with heresy and disobedience.

Immediately, Luther wrote a letter to his protector, Prince Frederick. Frederick admired and favored Luther because of the publicity Luther had attracted to Wittenberg. In the letter, Luther asked Frederick to promise not to

LUTHER REFUSES TO RECANT

Cardinal Cajetan, the pope's representative in Augsburg, expected only a brief interview with Luther. The cardinal was instructed not to discuss any of the issues raised by the so-called obstinate monk.

"My son," said the cardinal in a fatherly tone, "all I want you to do is say revoco — I recant!"

"Father," answered Luther humbly but firmly, "I didn't come all the way to Augsburg to do what I could just as well have done in Wittenberg. Please inform me of my errors."

Cajetan paused. He noticed the innocent look the question had left on Luther's face. Then he took a deep breath and overstepped his instructions. The discussion which followed lasted three days.

"Your main error," he began, "is that you deny a person will receive God's forgiveness in Christ by buying indulgences from the Church. This is against the teaching of the Church."

"But not against God's Word!" retorted Luther. "The Bible doesn't even mention indulgences. It states clearly that only by faith in Jesus Christ can we receive God's forgiveness."

"Your next error," continued Cajetan unmoved, "is that you deny the word of the pope is above the Bible."

"Yes. The Word of God is above any pope and any Church," exclaimed Luther.

allow any trial to take place outside of Germany. This would make it too easy for Luther's enemies to have him killed. If a hearing could be arranged on German soil, Luther wanted a promise of safe conduct from Emperor Maximilian himself.

A hearing was arranged in Augsburg. But Luther left for that place with a troubled heart. What would happen to him? How could he be sure he was right and everyone else wrong? With the pope, the emperor and the archbishop against him, he could hardly escape the guilty verdict, and would inevitably be burned at the stake.

"Now I must die!" he thought. "What a disgrace I shall be to my parents!"

"Let me remind you, my son, that the Bible has to be correctly interpreted. His Holiness, the pope, is the God-appointed interpreter."

"I say," spoke Luther, "that any humble Christian armed with the Word of God is a better interpreter than the pope."

"Will you also deny that the pope is Christ's representative on earth?"

"If the pope abuses Scripture as in the case of indulgences — then yes! Indulgences are only a scheme meant to raise money!"

The next day Luther handed Cajetan a written statement that

explained his view in detail.

"Thank you, I shall forward your letter to Rome," said the cardinal. Then he added, "But now it's time to recant. Just say revoco. That's all."

"I refuse to recant," declared Luther, "unless you convince me that I am wrong according to Scripture or with reason."

The cardinal's face grew red with rage. "Do you realize," he thundered, "I have orders to put you in chains and take you to Rome for trial if you do not recant! Don't appear before me again until you're ready to recant!"

Luther knew the verdict of Rome would be execution. He left Augsburg as fast as he could, and not through the city gate either, but through a hole in the city wall. Luther was running for his life.

"Cajetan was no more fit to handle the case than a donkey is fit to play on a harp."

—Luther

Understanding Luther's Enemies

JOHANN TETZEL was a short, fiery preacher of the Dominican order who was especially good at selling indulgences throughout Germany. In 1517, when the pope and the German archbishop needed extra money, Tetzel saw his chance to make use of his talents. In many German towns he preached his "indulgence gospel" of the forgiveness of sins: no repentance required, just money in Tetzel's trunk.

After being exposed by Luther as a crook, Tetzel was still granted the title of "Doctor of Theology" with the right to publish his writings. Immediately he fired off 106 theses against Luther. But contrary to his opponent, Tetzel was a poor theologian and thinker. He eventually lost the pope's favor.

The indulgence peddler retired to a monastery in Leipzig and was further disfavored for his luxurious lifestyle. He had two children out of wedlock, and the retirement income he had established for himself was said to be ten times higher than the Leipzig mayor's. Tetzel died a broken man, only two years after his lucrative career had begun. Before his death Luther wrote him: "Don't be too discouraged! You were not the one who started this madness."

POPE LEO X came from a prominent Italian family that managed to buy him status as a cardinal by the time he was thirteen. Twenty-five years later (1513) he was elected pontiff of the Roman Catholic Church.

Pope Leo was a sociable,

A TRIUMPHANT MARCH

Though on the run, Luther was a target Pope Leo wouldn't want to miss. When he spoke openly against the teaching of the Church, Luther had defied "His Holiness" himself. Luther was causing a national uprising in Germany that Leo knew might divide the Church and the entire empire.

Pope Leo was watching Luther's every move from Rome. When he heard that Luther had defended a

heretic, executed a hundred years before, he had the evidence he was looking for: Luther himself was a heretic!

Leo signed a document that threatened to excommunicate Luther from the Church unless he confessed his

> "This will be my recantation at Worms, 'I declare that the pope is the enemy of Christ and the apostle of the devil.'"
> —Luther

"errors" within 60 days. Luther replied by burning the bull, the document declaring him to be a heretic, together with the constitution of the Church. He even called the pope "Antichrist," enemy of Jesus.

This added fuel to the fire being

pleasure-loving and careless leader. On his coronation alone he spent 100,000 ducats — one seventh of the reserve in the papal treasury. His ambition to finish St. Peter's Cathedral in Rome would cost over a million ducats. After a few years Leo had exhausted his financial resources and was in serious trouble. New cash flow was needed.

In order to get money, Leo created thousands of new church offices and filled them with wealthy people in return for financial bribes. The Church was fast becoming a secular institution lacking spirituality.

Another important source of income was the sale of indulgences. Indulgences had been sold since the Crusades three hundred years earlier. Leo turned the practice into big business. He hoped to get enough money to start another crusade against the Muslim Turks.

Luther's attack on the indulgence trade was a threat to Leo's lifestyle. Leo's condemnation of Luther in 1520 was based on ulterior motives, rather than spiritual ones. However, Leo was forced to

send out a document, Cum Postquam (1518), that complied with Luther's views and corrected the worst abuses.

In 1521, after having won a battle with the French, Leo celebrated his triumph with a great banquet. That night he caught a cold and soon afterwards died .

At his funeral, half-burned candles borrowed from another funeral were used because the papacy was so deeply in debt. During his seven years in office, Leo had spent five million ducats.

JOHANN ECK was a fellow professor at the university of Ingolstadt and a good friend of Luther until the indulgence controversy broke out. From that time on Eck organized the opposition prepared for Luther in Rome. But Luther had slowly come to realize he was giving voice to the longings of an entire nation. There was no turning back. If he recanted now, he would go against the Bible and his conscience — and that would make him a heretic in the eyes of God. Luther could only preach and write on, refusing to go to Rome, hoping for a fair hearing under the Roman emperor and resting his case with Almighty God.

Twenty-year-old Charles, the new emperor who followed Maximilian, had just been elected by Germany's seven princes, of whom Luther's protector, Frederick the Wise, was the most influential. Frederick convinced Charles that Luther deserved at least a trial. If the emperor's council found Luther guilty of heresy, Frederick promised to be the first to condemn him.

The occasion for a trial came in 1521 during the emperor's first national Council in Worms, Germany. Luther was granted safe conduct and escorted by the emperor's herald and guard on the long journey from Wittenberg.

Everywhere people flocked into the streets to see Luther and encourage him. At Leipzig he was honored by the town council and given gifts. At Erfurt he was greeted with music and speeches. The professors and students at his old university lined up to honor him.

After two weeks of triumphant traveling, Luther finally arrived in

against Luther.

In 1519, George, the duke of Saxony, arranged a public debate between Eck and Luther. Eck was a professional debater who wanted to corner his former friend. The debate lasted eighteen days, and Eck managed to convince the audience that Luther was a heretic like John Hus, a reformer from Bohemia who had been burned at the stake one hundred years earlier.

The papal document, or bull, that condemned Luther as a heretic in 1520 was most likely drafted by Eck. Luther called it "the work of that man of lies, hypocrisy, errors, heresy — that monster Johann Eck." Still, Eck did not succeed in destroying Luther.

CHARLES I of Spain was elected Holy Roman Emperor in 1519, at age nineteen. His empire covered most of Europe. Though Charles had many enemies (including France, the pope and the Turks), his most urgent problem was the Protestant uprising that threatened to split apart his empire.

After the Council at Worms (1521), Charles banned Luther with the words, "A single monk who goes against the Christianity of a thousand years must be wrong."

But Charles never pursued his decision to destroy Luther. Other political problems preoccupied him until he finally lost control of his territories. The Protestant princes forced him to accept their right to determine the religion of their own countries.

Charles abdicated the throne in 1556 and retired to a monastery. In his hour of death his last word was, "Jesus."

Worms. His arrival was announced by the town trumpeter. Luther turned to the friends who were with him and said, "Now I've had my triumphant Palm Sunday. What comes next may be my Calvary."

The hearing was scheduled for 4 p.m. the following day.

BEFORE THE EMPEROR

Luther entered the hall in the palace and stood before the emperor, who sat on his throne. Around him were princes, noblemen, bishops and distinguished officials from many states and cities throughout Germany. The contrast between the richly clothed medieval dignitaries and the simple monk in a coarse robe, confidently challenging the religious system of his day, marked the beginning of modern times.

"Martin Luther," began an official, pointing at a pile of books in the middle of the room, "have you written these?"

Luther did not answer.

The official read the titles out loud and asked again, "Have you written these books?"

"Yes," answered Luther, "and I have written others, too."

"Is there anything in your books," questioned the official, "that you want to recant?"

Luther was confused. What was this? He had come to Worms in the hope that he would be asked about his views, but all he was being asked was Cajetan's old question. Had the council already judged him?

"This," he stammered, "touches God and His Word—and the salvation of souls. Please give me time to think it over."

Next day, when Luther was finally led into the hall, the dark room was lit with candles. The official repeated the question from the previous day. Did Luther regret anything in the books he had written? The emperor and the princes leaned forward anx-iously. Prince Frederick looked pale. The pope's ambassador had a face of stone. Luther took a deep breath and said with a clear voice,

"There are three kinds of books in the pile. The first kind deal with faith and life so simply that no one will object to them. I cannot retract any of those, of course.

"The second kind of books," he continued, "attack the pope and his teaching. I cannot withdraw those either, since I won't support tyranny.

"Finally there are books attacking others. I may have been harsh in my judgments, but cannot renounce any of these without encouraging the ungodliness these men represent.

"I ask you to show me my errors. If you do, I'll be the first to throw my books into the fire."

"Martin," objected the official, "how can you assume you are right and the Church wrong for a thousand years? Please answer my question simply: Do you or do you not renounce your books and the errors in them?"

Luther's answer has become a classic one, "Unless I'm convinced on the grounds of Scripture or by plain reason, I cannot and will not recant. My conscience is captive to the Word of God. It's neither safe nor wise to act against one's conscience." Then he bowed his head and said in a low voice, "Here I stand. I can do no other. God help me! Amen."

Three Important Books by Luther

More books have been written about Martin Luther than any other individual in history — except for Jesus Christ.

Luther himself wrote many books and pamphlets (about 60,000 pages!). His enemies did what they could to ban and burn his books, but the success of the Reformation was greatly due to these books. Still Luther said, "I wish all my books would disappear and the Holy Scriptures alone be read."

Three of the reformer's early books are most important to the Reformation:

• **ADDRESS TO THE CHRISTIAN NOBILITY** (1520). Luther encouraged the German leaders to take on the responsibility of reform since the Roman Catholic Church barricaded itself against change.

• **THE BABYLONIAN CAPTIVITY OF THE CHURCH** (1520). The title refers to the exile of the Jews in Babylon (586 BC). Luther claimed the people of God in his own day were led away from Scripture and held captive by the pope and the papal system. Luther also reduced the traditional seven sacraments to two: Baptism and Communion. He denied that the bread and the wine are transformed into the actual Body and Blood of Jesus and suggested that lay people receive the wine as well as the bread.

• **ON THE FREEDOM OF A CHRISTIAN** (1520). This powerful book turned the repressive medieval view of man upside down. Luther's main idea was that true freedom has two sides: A Christian is lord of all, subject to no one, and a Christian is a dutiful servant of all, subject to everyone. Luther said this book "contains, in a nutshell, the whole of the Christian life."

KIDNAPPED!

Several days passed while the officials tried to negotiate with Luther. But he would not change his mind. Finally he was allowed to go home before his period of safe conduct ran out. The emperor forbade him to preach or write new books until a decision had been reached.

Luther obeyed—almost. On his way northeast towards Wittenberg he did accept a few invitations to preach, one of which was in Eisenach, where he had spent the happiest years of his childhood.

It was late afternoon by the time Luther and his few companions had left Eisenach and were making their way down a lonely road through the dark woods. Suddenly, a group of armed horsemen came out of nowhere and forced the wagon to stop.

"Which of you is Martin Luther?" demanded one of the horsemen. The wagon driver panicked and pointed at Martin. The men dragged Luther from the wagon and mounted him on a horse. Then they disappeared with him the same way they had come. Luther's companions fled on foot.

Soon rumors of Luther's kidnapping spread throughout Germany and

beyond. Some thought he'd been taken to Rome to be burned. Others said he'd been killed in the forest by the emperor's men. Everyone knew the emperor had sided with the pope and declared Luther an outlaw. This meant anyone could kill him without being charged for murder. Luther's friends were shocked. One of them, the artist Albrecht Durer, wrote from The Netherlands, "O God, if he is dead, who will then explain to us the gospel? If we lose this man who has written more clearly than any other in centuries, may God raise up another."

> "I wish my name may be passed over in silence, and that people will call themselves not Lutheran but Christian."
> —Luther

"PRISONER" AT WARTBURG

But Luther was perfectly safe. From the forest he had been taken to Wartburg, one of Prince Frederick's castles. The kidnapping scene had in fact been arranged by Frederick himself.

For the next ten months Luther was held "prisoner" at Wartburg. He was given a beautiful room with a retractable stairway, fine meals and clothes fit for a knight.

Knight Jorg, as Luther was now called, had plenty of time to think about the movement he had started. With its leader condemned both by Church and state, it looked as though his mission had failed. Could the movement go on without him? How could he best make sure it took a just and peaceful course? He wanted a reformation of the Church, not a bloody revolution. The German peasants were restless and could very well turn his cause into civil war.

"I would rather burn on live coals than rot here without being able to do anything," he thought—overwhelmed by discouragement and depression.

Then he sat down and began to write. The next ten months were to be the most productive in his life. The twelve books he wrote at Wartburg contain the pastoral consequences of his theology. He also translated the New Testament from Greek into German in only eleven weeks. This translation, Luther's gift to his beloved people, helped form a common German language.

"A Mighty Fortress"

In 1527, when the Black Plague struck Wittenberg, Luther became seriously ill. Depressed, he wrote his friend, Philip Melanchton, "I spent more than a week in death and in hell. Completely abandoned by Christ, I struggled with depression and blasphemy against God. But through the prayers of the saints, God began to have mercy on me and pulled my soul from the inferno below."

In the midst of his depression, Luther wrote and composed the powerful hymn, A Mighty Fortress, about the faithfulness of God. Verses 1 and 3 read:

A mighty fortress is our God,
A bulwark never failing;
Our helper He, amid the flood
Of mortal ills prevailing.
For still our ancient foe
Does seek to work us woe;
His craft and power are great,
And, armed with cruel hate,
On earth is not his equal.

And though this world, with devils filled
Should threaten to undo us,
We will not fear, for God has willed
His truth to triumph through us.
The prince of darkness grim —
We tremble not for him;
His rage we can endure,
For lo! his doom is sure,
One little word shall fell him.

LUTHER'S LATER YEARS

After Wartburg, Luther lived another 25 years, although he remained banned by the emperor and the pope. Under his leadership, the Reformation Church,

nicknamed the Protestants, grew healthy and strong. By his death in 1546, the movement had spread to all the countries of northern Europe and set the stage for a nationalism that refuted the emperor and the Catholic Church.

At the core of the Protestant Church's beliefs was the absolute authority of the Bible and faith in Jesus Christ as the only Way of salvation. Instead of the hierarchy of pope,

Luther's Wife Katie

"I believe in marriage," said Luther repeatedly. He encouraged the monks and nuns who fled the cloisters because of his teaching to get married.

Katharina von Bora and eight other nuns showed up on Luther's doorstep one day, smuggled out of their Cistercian convent on a wagon with barrels of beer and herring. Luther felt responsible for their future and found husbands for seven of them. When only Katharina was left, she refused to marry anyone but Luther or one of his close friends.

Two years later, in 1525, Luther and Katie were married in the Wittenberg church. She was 26. He was 42. The prince gave them the Black Cloister, Luther's former monastery, for a home. The house was always full of people who needed spiritual or physical help. The dinner table usually had 20-30 people seated around it.

Katie was an excellent wife with common sense in practical matters that her husband often lacked. Luther was fond of her and called her "my lord." Together they had six children and adopted four.

cardinals, bishops and priests, the Protestant Church claimed the "priesthood of all believers," or every Christian's right and responsibility to minister to other Christians, interpret the Scriptures and represent Christ among unbelievers. The Church, or at least part of it, had finally come back to the teachings of the first-century Church.

Luther's death occurred while on a business trip to Eisleben, where he had been born and baptized. On February 17th, 1546, at age 63, he went to bed with chest pains. At 1 a.m. he cried,

> "I don't want people to fight on the side of the gospel with force and killing. The world is to be won over with the Word of God."
>
> —Luther

"Oh Lord God, the pain is unbearable!" As companions rushed into the chamber they heard their leader repeat words from the Gospel of John, "For God so loved the world that He gave His only Son . . . ."

"Reverend Father," a friend broke in, "do you stand firm in Christ and the teachings you've preached?"

"Yes," answered Luther in a faint voice. Then he was dead.

Today, more than 450 years after his death, Martin Luther is considered by many, to be the most important church teacher since the apostle Paul.

Main Events in Luther's Life

1483	10 Dec.	Born in Eisleben.
1484	June	Family moves to Mansfeld.
1497	Easter	Latin school in Magdeburg.
1498		St. George's school in Eisenach.
1501	May	University of Erfurt.
1502	29 Dec.	Receives Bachelor of Arts degree.
1503	16 April	Seriously wounded by sword.
1505	7 Jan.	Receives Master of Arts degree.
	20 May	Begins law studies.
	2 July	Thunderstorm and vow.
	17 July	Enters Augustinian monastery in Erfurt.
1507	3 April	Ordained priest.
	2 May	First Mass.
1508	Winter	Teaches philosophy at Wittenberg.
1510	Nov.	Pilgrimage to Rome.
1511	April	Returns to Erfurt.
1512	19 Oct.	Transfers to Wittenberg. Doctor of Theology.
1513–1516		Lectures on Psalms, Romans and Galatians.
1517	31 Oct.	Posts the 95 theses.
1518	5 Aug.	Maximilian warns Pope Leo.
	7 Aug.	Summoned to Rome.
	8 Aug.	Appeal to Frederick.
	12 Oct.	Hearing before Cajetan at Augsburg.
	20 Oct.	Flight from Augsburg.
1519	July	The Leipzig debate with Dr. Eck.
1520	15 June	Pope's bull. Luther has 60 days to recant.
	12 Nov.	Luther's books burned at Cologne.
	10 Dec.	Luther burns Pope's bull at Wittenberg.
1521	3 Jan.	Excommunicated from the Church.
1521	16 April	Arrives at Council in Worms.
	26 April	Leaves Worms.
	4 May	Arrives at Wartburg.
	Dec.	Begins translation of the New Testament.
1522	6 March	Returns to Wittenberg.
1525	5 May	Death of Frederick the Wise.
	June	Peasant uprising crushed.
	13 June	Marriage to Katharina von Bora.
1527	Aug.	Sick and depressed. "A Mighty Fortress."
1530	June	Diet of Augsburg.
1534		Completes German Bible.
1546	18 Feb.	Dies in Eisleben.

BOOK RESOURCES

Here I Stand: A Life of Martin Luther, by Ronald Bainton (Abingdon, 1977).

Martin Luther, by Mike Fearon (Bethany, 1986).

Luther the Reformer, by James Kittelson (Augsburg, 1986).

Martin Luther: The Man and His Work, by Arthur McGiffert (Century, 1911).

Martin Luther, by McNeer and Ward (Abingdon, 1953).

Luther: His Life and Work, by Gerhard Ritter (Harper & Row, 1963).

Christian History, Issue 34, 1992: Martin Luther: The Early Years.

LUTHER'S GERMANY

Magdeburg

Elbe

Wittenberg

Eisleben

Mansfeld

Weser

Fulda

Eisenach

Wartburg

Erfurt

Jena

Leipzig

Saale

Frankfurt

Worms

Rhein

Nuremberg

Neckar

Donau

Miles

10 20 30 40

Augsburg